Library of Congress Control Number: 2017955789

ISBN 978-93-89823-98-1

Edited by Cassandra Pelham Fulton
Book design by Kazu Kibuishi and Phil Falco
Creative Director: David Saylor
First edition, October 2018

This edition: November 2022

Printed in India

AMULET

KAZU KIBUISHI

BOOK EIGHT
SUPERNOVA

AN IMPRINT OF
SCHOLASTIC

3

4

7

THE CITY OF IPPO, IN THE NATION OF LUFEN

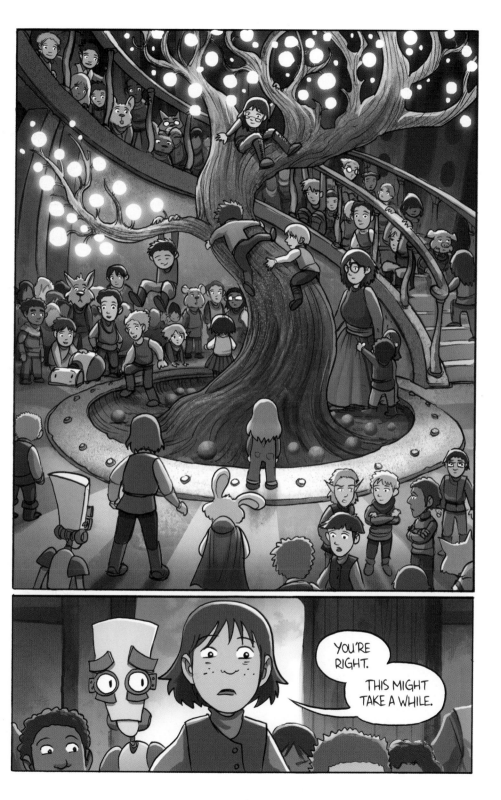

YOU'RE RIGHT.

THIS MIGHT TAKE A WHILE.

17

27

35

41

HWEEEEEEE

BOOM!!

43

49

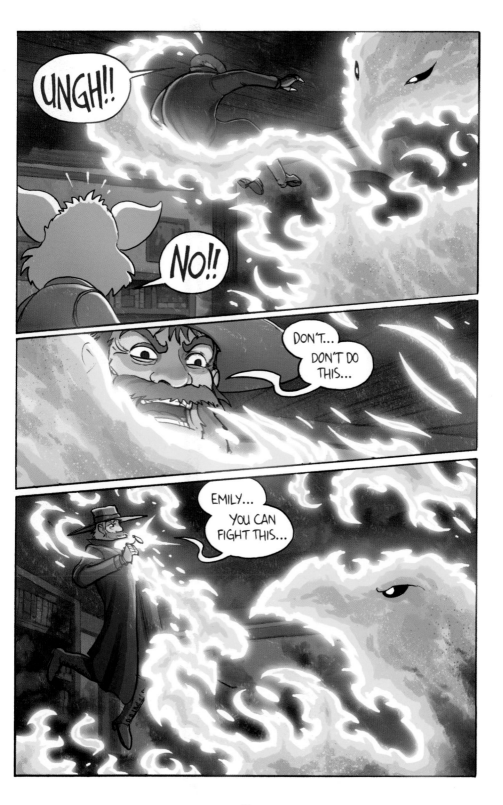

58

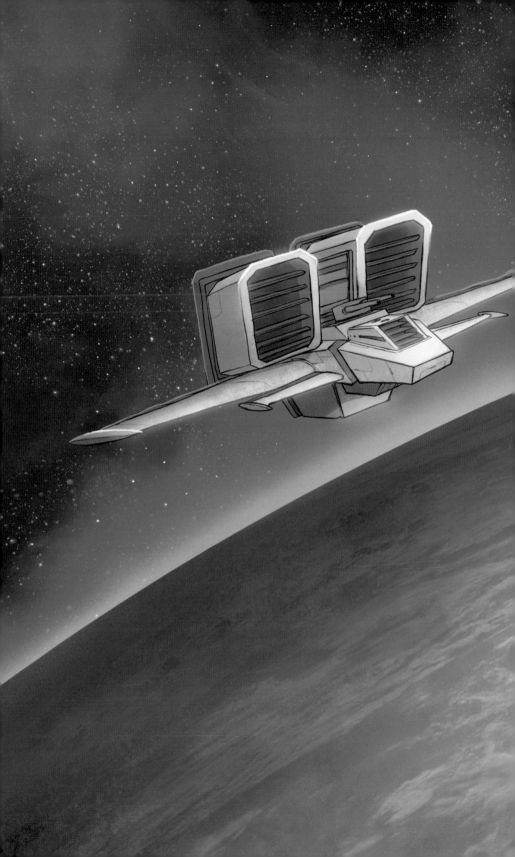

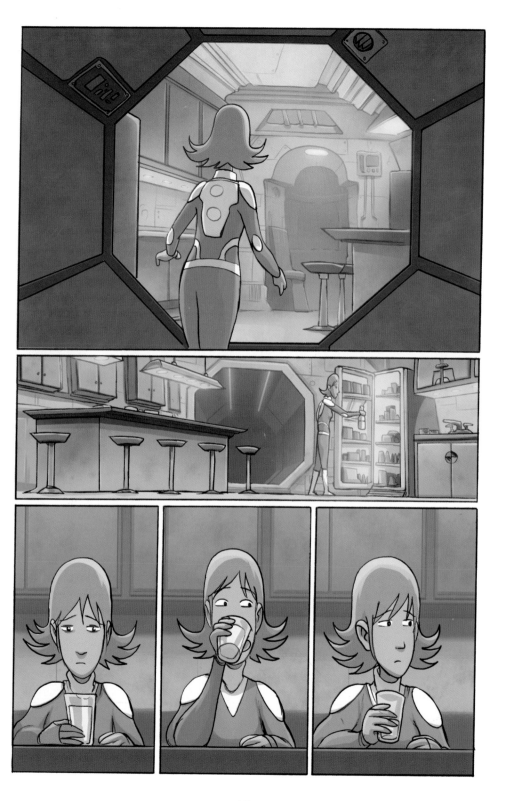

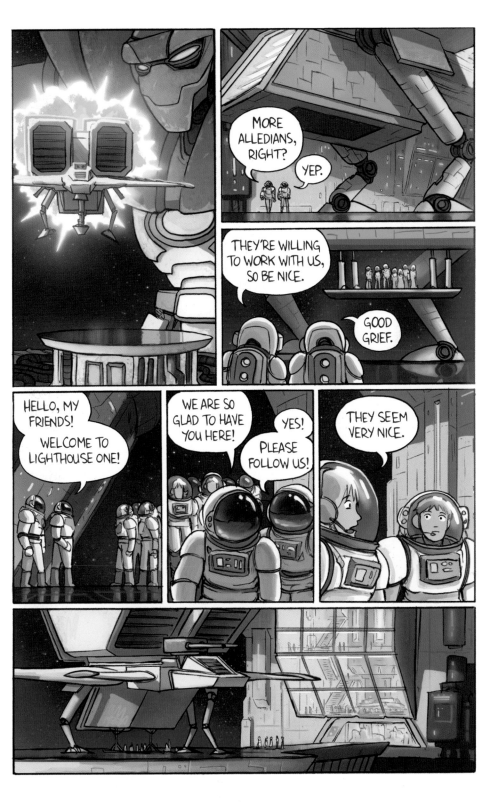

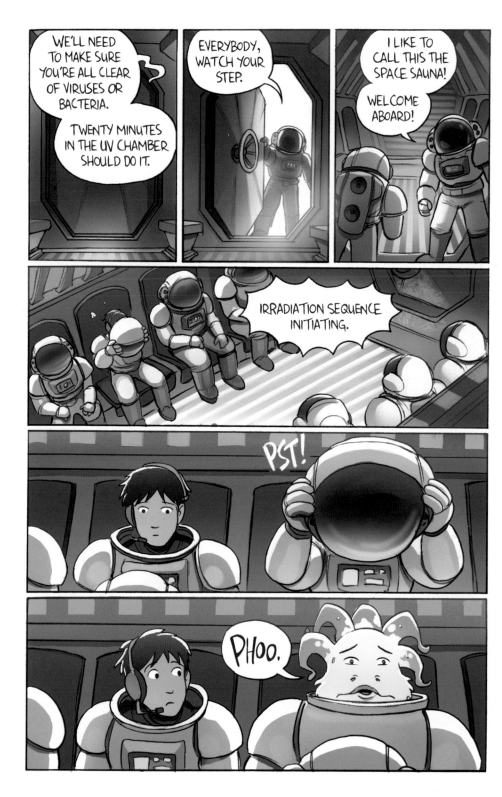

74

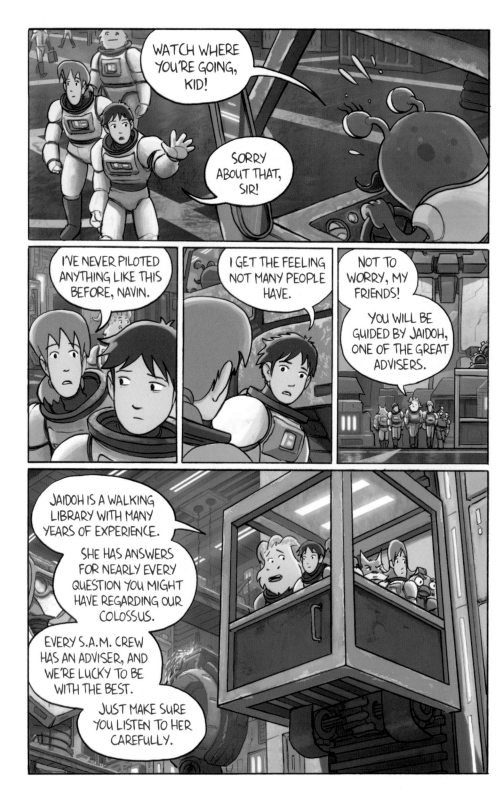

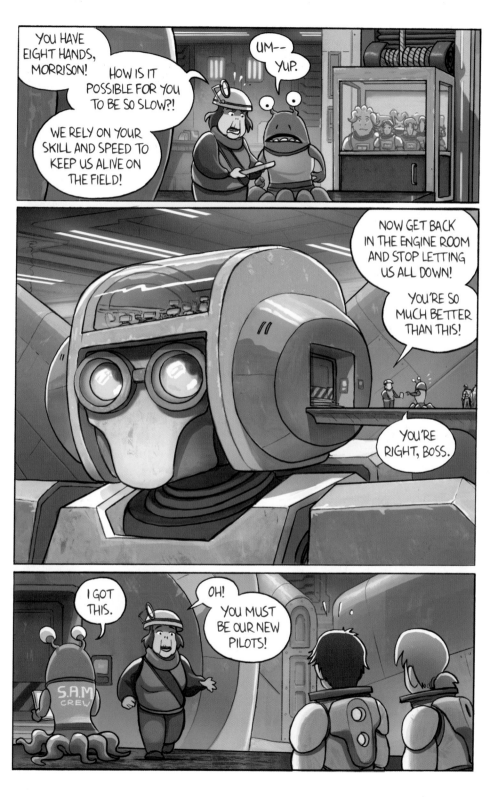

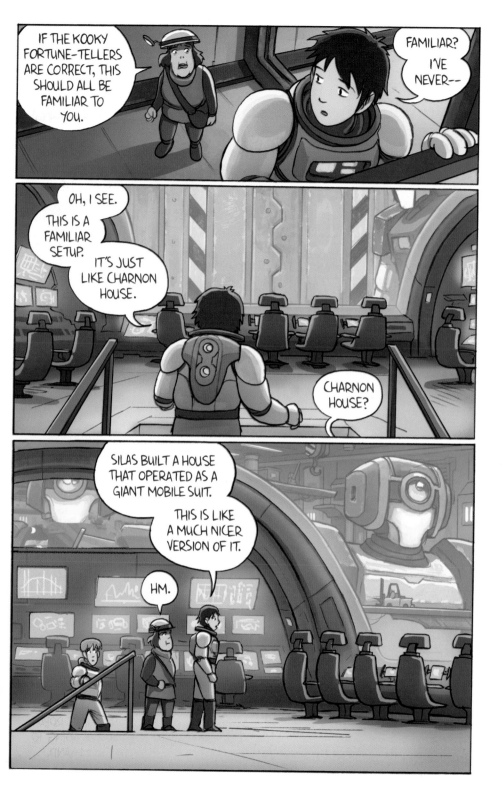

83

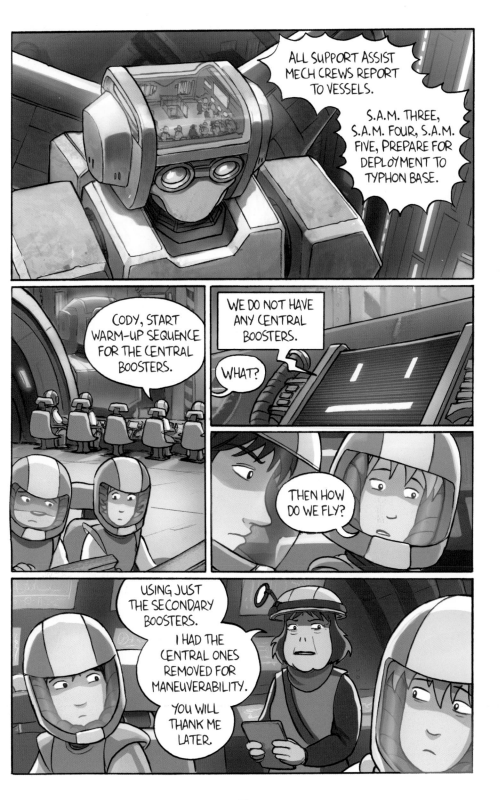

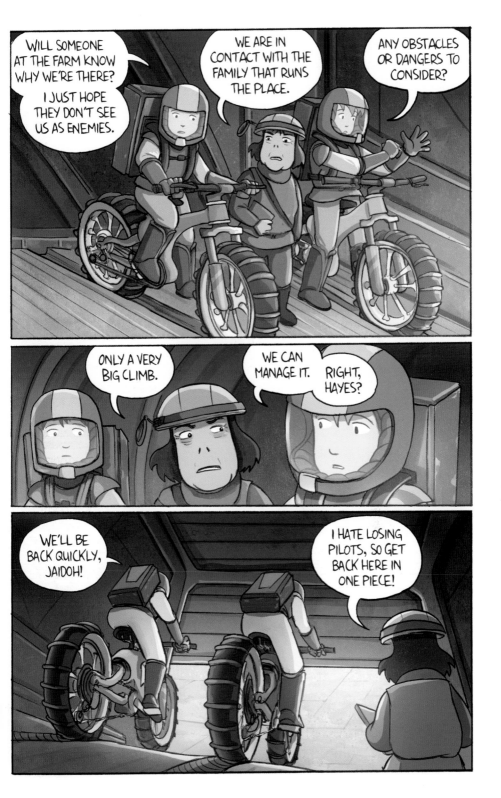

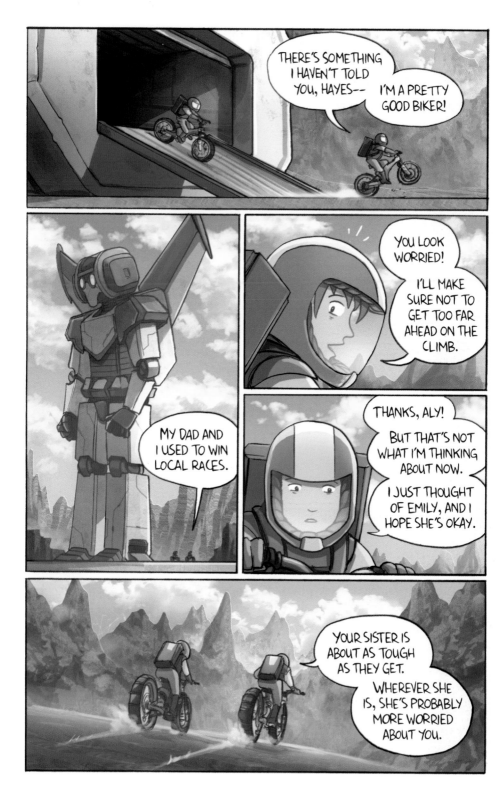

THIS CHAMBER IS A QUIET SPACE FREQUENTLY VISITED BY SOME OF OUR NEWER STONEKEEPERS.

MOZE, THIS IS EMILY. SHE'S ALSO NEW HERE.

LIKE YOUNG MOZE HERE.

HELLO, EMILY.

HELLO, MOZE.

WANT TO JOIN ME ON THE TREE ISLAND?

TREE ISLAND?

IT'S MY FAVORITE PLACE TO SPEND TIME AROUND HERE.

IT'S NICE.

COME ON. I'LL SHOW YOU WHERE IT IS.

THANK YOU, MOZE.

YOU'RE WELCOME.

THE NIGHT FOUR STONEKEEPERS LOST CONTROL OF THEIR POWERS...
AND CHANGED THE COURSE OF ALLEDIAN HISTORY.
I KNOW THIS STORY.
MY GREAT-GRANDFATHER SILAS CHARNON HELPED FIGHT THEM OFF.
STONEKEEPERS LIKE HIM SAVED ALLEDIA.

YOU MADE IT THROUGH!

AND YOU HAVE NOT AGED ALL THAT MUCH.

VERY GOOD.

YOU'RE THE LADY I MET IN THE VOID PRISON.

PRISON?

OH, THE VOID IS NOT A PRISON.

IT IS A SPACE AWAY FROM YOUR WORLD THAT GIVES YOU TIME TO THINK.

IT IS A PLACE TO REFLECT.

DURING DIFFICULT TIMES IN YOUR LIFE, YOU MAY NEED TO RETURN TO THIS PLACE TO RESET YOURSELF.

COME ON, I'LL HELP YOU GET BACK TO ALLEDIA.

EMILY!

MOZE!

I FOUND THE PORTAL.

BUT WE MUST MOVE QUICKLY.

I THINK THE SHADOWS SPOTTED ME COMING HERE.

I HOPE YOU'RE COMFORTABLE FLYING.

LET'S GO!

I CAN MANAGE.

WE MAY HAVE TO FIGHT OUR WAY THROUGH THEM.

I'M FROM THE CITY OF CIELIS ON ALLEDIA.

NAVIN IS FROM THE PLANET EARTH.

HAVE THE SHADOWS CAUSED PROBLEMS ON YOUR PLANETS?

YES. MANY OF OUR CITIES ARE UNDER SIEGE FROM THE SHADOWS.

MY SISTER FOUND ONE ON EARTH.

WHEN YOU SEE ONE, YOU CAN BE SURE THERE ARE MANY MORE OF THEM.

PRETTY SOON, THE PLANET WILL BE OVERRUN BY SHADOWS.

YOU SAID YOU HAVE A SISTER.

WHAT'S HER NAME?

EMILY.

WHERE IS EMILY NOW?

SHE'S STILL ON ALLEDIA.

WORKING TO RESTORE THE GUARDIAN COUNCIL.

YOUR SISTER IS A STONEKEEPER?

DO YOU KNOW WHAT HAPPENS WHEN THEY LOSE CONTROL OF THEIR POWERS?

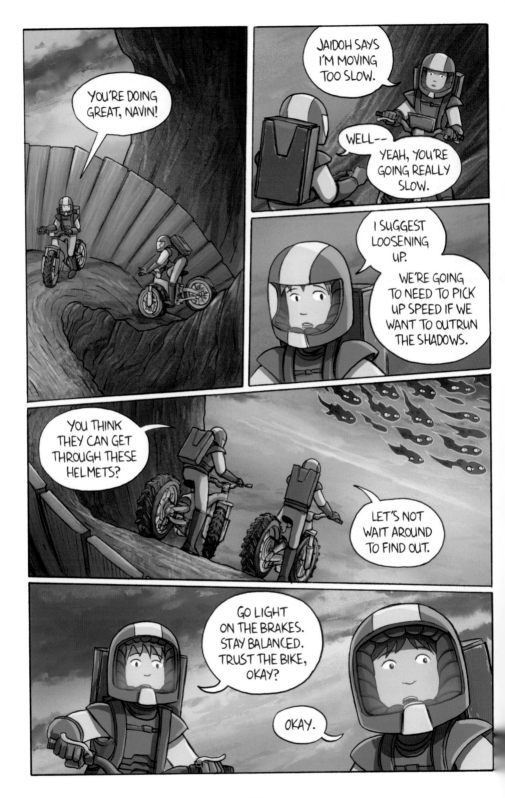

171

173

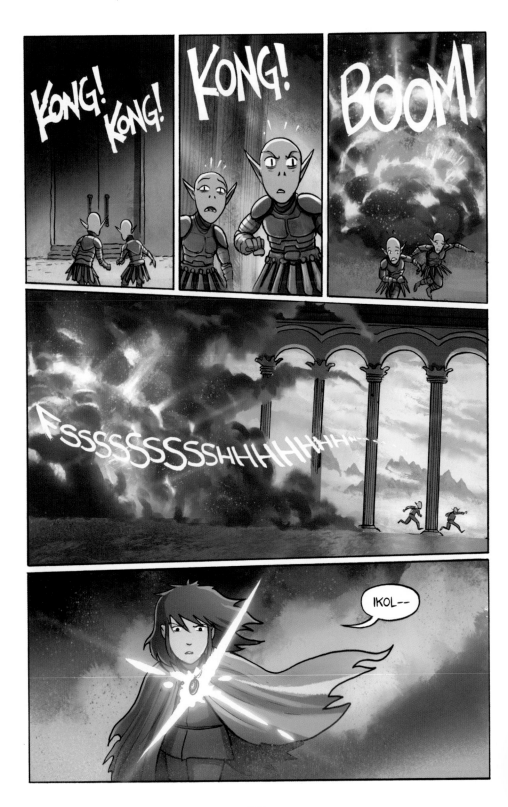

TO BE CONCLUDED IN BOOK NINE...

CREATED AT

BOLT CITY
PRODUCTIONS

WRITTEN & ILLUSTRATED BY
KAZU KIBUISHI

LEAD PRODUCTION ASSISTANT
JASON CAFFOE

COLORS & BACKGROUNDS BY
JASON CAFFOE
KAZU KIBUISHI
AMY KIM KIBUISHI
FORREST DICKISON
TIM PROBERT
POLYNA KIM
AUDRA ANN FURUICHI
DERICK TSAI
AMANDA JANE SHARPE
JOE MARQUIS
KELLY HAMILTON

PAGE FLATTING
CRYSTAL KAN
MEGAN BRENNAN
POLYNA KIM
JOEY HAN
AUDRA ANN FURUICHI
LINDSEY REIMER
PRESTON DO

SPECIAL THANKS
Judith Hansen, Cassandra Pelham Fulton, Phil Falco, David Saylor,
Nancy Caffoe, Juni & Sophie Kibuishi, Rachel & Hazel Caffoe,
Dan & Heidi Ullom, Moses Phillips, Bart Foutch, and Ryan Brown
and the Bicycle Centres crew.

Thank you to all the librarians, booksellers, parents, and readers
for whom this book was made.

ABOUT THE AUTHOR

Kazu Kibuishi is the creator of the #1 *New York Times* bestselling Amulet series, which is available in 16 languages. *Amulet, Book One: The Stonekeeper* was an ALA Best Book for Young Adults and a Children's Choice Book Award finalist. He is also the creator of *Copper*, a collection of his popular webcomic that features an adventuresome boy-and-dog pair. Kazu also illustrated the covers of the 15th anniversary paperback editions of the Harry Potter series written by J.K. Rowling. He lives and works near Seattle, Washington, with his wife, Amy Kim Kibuishi, and their children.

Visit Kazu online at www.boltcity.com.